THE
HOLY GHOST

St. Didymas the Blind,
Dean of the Catechetical School of Alexandria

Translated by: D.P. Curtin

Dalcassian Publishing Company
PHILADELPHIA, PA

THE HOLY GHOST

Copyright @ 2008 Dalcassian Publishing Company

All rights reserved. No part of this publication may be reproduced, distributed, or transmitted in any form or by any means, including photocopying, recording, or other electronic or mechanical methods, without the prior written permission of the publisher, except in the case of brief quotations embodied in critical reviews and certain other non-commercial uses permitted by copyright law. For permission request, write to Dalcassian Publishing Company at dalcassianpublishing at gmail.com

ISBN: 979-8-8689-9123-3 (Paperback)

Library of Congress Control Number:
Author: Curtin, D.P. (1985-)

Printed by Ingram Content Group, 1 Ingram Blvd, La Vergne, Tennessee

First printing edition 2008.

THE HOLY GHOST

THE HOLY GHOST

THE HOLY GHOST

THE TWO BOOKS OF THE ALEXANDRIAN, ON THE HOLY SPIRIT, AS INTERPRETED BY ST. JEROME.

1. Indeed, we must pay attention to all things that are divine with reverence and intense care; the Holy Spirit is called divinity: especially when the blasphemy against him is without pardon: so that the punishment of the blasphemer is aimed at, not only for every present age, but also for the future. Indeed, the Savior says that there is no forgiveness for the blasphemer against the Holy Spirit, neither in this world nor in the future (Mark 3). Wherefore it is more and more necessary to consider what the Scriptures relate to him, lest the error of blasphemy should sneak up on anyone, at least through ignorance. It would indeed have been expedient for a faithful and timid man, controlling his powers, to pass over the greatness of the present question in silence, and not to draw the matter full of danger into his crisis. It is true that some, rather than the right way, are raised to heaven, and boast of these things about the Holy Spirit, which were neither read in the Scriptures, nor used by any of the ancient Ecclesiastics, we are compelled to yield to the frequent exhortation of the brethren; to prove it by evidence: lest those who oppose the opposites be deceived by the ignorance of so great a dogma, who, without careful discussion, are at once drawn into the opinions of their adversaries.

2. The appellation of the Holy Spirit, and that which is shown by the substance of the appellation itself, is completely unknown to those who philosophize outside the sacred Scriptures. For only in our letters, and its concept and term are referred to, both in the new and in the old. Indeed, the man of the Old Testament, David, a participant in its effect, prayed that it might continue in him, saying: Take not your Holy Spirit from me (Psal. L). God is said to have the Holy Spirit, as though already dwelling in him. Nor even in the New Testament are these men who are described as having pleased God, filled with the Holy Spirit. For John, sanctified while still in his mother's womb, exults, and Jesus, rising from the dead, when he breathed into the face of the disciples, said: Receive the Holy Spirit (Luke 1). The volumes of the divine Scriptures are full of these words, which I have collected in the present work, and I have sat down to digest them: because it is not difficult, from what we have assumed, to find each reader similar to himself.

3. But let no one suspect that there was another Holy Spirit into the holy men before the coming of the Lord, and another in the apostles and the rest of the disciples, and as if homonymous in different substances. Bearing witness to the volume, he mentions that it was said by the Holy Spirit: And as the Holy Spirit says: Today if you will hear his voice, do not harden your hearts, etc. (Hebrews 3:7, from Psalm 94:8). Also, in the Acts of the Apostles, arguing with the Jews, he says: As the Holy Spirit spoke through Isaiah the prophet to our fathers, saying: You will hear a rumor and not understand (Acts 3). among the Prophets before the coming of the Lord there was another: but of him of which he himself was a partaker: and all who were carried in the faith of consummated virtue. Whence he mentions in his article, as if contesting that he was solitary and one, where he says not simply. Πνεῦμα ἅγιον, this is Holy Spirit, but with the addition of the article τὸ Πνεῦμα τὸ ἅγιον: this is the Holy Spirit. , by which he persuaded those present: It was necessary, he said, to fulfill the Scripture which the Holy Spirit spoke (that is, τὸ Πνεῦμα τὸ ἅγιον) through the mouth of David of Judah (Acts 1, 16): showing himself the same Spirit, and it worked in the prophets and in the apostles. The very voice of the Holy Spirit is not an empty appellation, but demonstrative of the subjacent essence: associated with the Father and the Son, and completely alien from creatures. For when creatures are divided into visible and invisible, that is, into corporeal and incorporeal, neither is the Holy Spirit of corporeal substances, the inhabitant of

the soul and sense, the producer of speech and wisdom and knowledge: neither of invisible creatures. For all these things are capable of wisdom and other virtues, and of sanctification. This substance, of which we are now speaking, is the producer of wisdom and knowledge and sanctification. Nor can any fortitude be found in the Holy Spirit, or the operation of sanctification and virtue. Describing the place of the Gospel, Matthew and Luke, one of them says: How much more will the heavenly Father give good things to those who ask him (Matthew 5:11)? The other is true: How much more will your heavenly Father give his Holy Spirit to those who ask him (Luke 11:13)? to whom it appears that the Holy Spirit is the fullness of gifts of God: and those things which are divinely administered cannot subsist without him; because all benefits which are received by the grace of God's gifts derive from this source. Now that which is substantially good cannot be capable of external goodness, since it itself bestows the goodness of others. Therefore, it is manifest, not only from corporeal, but also from incorporeal creatures that it is alien to be the Holy Spirit; because the other substances receive this substance of sanctification: but this one is not only not capable of the sanctification of another, but is moreover the giver and creator. making an insult (Heb. 10:29), there is no doubt that he who, after receiving it, sinned. But if he was sanctified through the communion of the Holy Spirit, it is shown that he himself was a partaker of it, and the benefactor of his sanctification, the Holy Spirit. The Apostle also writing to the Corinthians, and enumerating those who will attain the kingdom of heaven, he adds saying: And these things indeed you were: but you were washed, but you were sanctified, but you were justified, in the name of Jesus Christ and in the Spirit of our God (1 Cor. 6, 11)., asserting that there is no other than the Holy Spirit. Indeed, in the consequences, he approves the same, saying: No one speaking in the Spirit of God says anathema to Jesus: and no one says Lord Jesus, except in the Holy Spirit (1 Cor. 12:3); Confirming that the Spirit of God is the Holy Spirit.

5. If therefore the sanctifier is not changeable but is shown of an unchangeable substance. But the immutable substance of God alone, and of his only begotten Son, is most clearly conveyed by the divine words: preaching the changeable and changeable substance of all creatures. it will be of the creature ὁμούσιον. For it would also be an unchangeable creature if it were placed with the Father and the Son, having the same invariability. For everything that is capable of alien

good is separated from this substance. But such are all creatures: but since God is good, he is the source and principle of good; He therefore makes those good to whom he imparts himself, the good itself not being made by another, but subsisting: therefore capable, and not capable. and he is not sanctified, but he sanctifies. Whence he himself is capable, and not capable. Therefore, since an invisible creature, which it is customary to call a rational and incorporeal substance, is not capable, but capable: for if he were capable, he would be capable of no good, though she herself is simple, subsisting, and the recipient of another's good: she should have good by participation, and not of those things which are possessed by others, but of those which others have; but a creature having, and not dwelling. and let it not take otherwise, and now, and we have expressed it in the volume of Sectaries (as we were able): and it is very easy to affirm our discourse from all Scripture. ours (Ephesians 1:13). For if some are sealed with the Holy Spirit, assuming his form and appearance: of these is the Holy Spirit, which they have and do not have: those who have it are sealed with his seal. Writing the same thing to the Corinthians, he says, do not grieve the Holy Spirit, in whom you are a sign (Ephes. 4, 30); contending that those who had received the communion of the Holy Spirit were sealed. For just as the one who receives instruction and virtue receives the seal and form (so to speak) into his sense of the knowledge which he has received: so also, he who is made a partaker of the Holy Spirit is made by his communion spiritual as well as holy.

6. The Holy Spirit himself, if he were one of the creatures, would at least have a circumscribed substance; like all things that have been made. For even if invisible creatures are not limited by place and ends, they are nevertheless limited by the property of substance. But the Holy Spirit, being in many, has no limited substance. and blowing into their faces: Receive, he said, the Holy Spirit, and as you go, teach all nations (John 20:22): as if he had sent all to all nations. into Scythia, and others scattered into other nations; according to the dispensation of him whom the Holy Spirit had with them, just as the Lord said: I am with you always, until the end of the age (Matthew 28:20). and you will be my witnesses in Jerusalem, and in all Judea and Samaria, and even to the ends of the earth (Acts 1:8). according to the testimony of the Lord, they were separated from each other by very long distances, but the indwelling Holy Spirit was present to them, having an uncircumscribed substance, an angelic power is shown to be completely different from this. For the angel who was

present, for example, to the Apostle in Asia praying, could not be present at the same time but the Holy Spirit is not only available to men separated from himself, but also to each and every angel, principality, throne, and dominion he inhabits. so also sanctifying other creatures, another of them is substance: since every creature is made holy, not from its own substance, but from the communion of another's holiness. of the Father, and of the holy angels (Luke 9:29). And Cornelius is written in the Acts of the Apostles by the holy angel it is submitted] that he received an answer (Acts 10:22) to call Peter to himself a disciple of Christ. It is true that angels are holy by the participation of the Holy Spirit, and by their indwelling of the only begotten Son of God, who is holiness, and the communion of the Father. About whom the Savior says: Holy Father (John 17:11). for as the Father who sanctifies is different from those who are sanctified: and the Son is different from those whom he makes holy. So also, the Holy Spirit is another substance from those whom he sanctifies by his own bestowal. Consequently, they are forced to say that ὁμουσίους is the Trinity, and that they are irreversibly holy according to their substance. to be of substance; whereas these have sanctity through the communion of the Trinity, and the angels, by their own holy nature, are alien from it. , and announcing to them the greater benefits of God. From which it is clearly shown that angels are more honorable and much better than men, through a more German, so to speak, and fuller assumption of the Trinity. of nature, with the rest of the creatures that receive him. But if he is of another nature from creatures, and subsists in his own essence, he is shown uncreated and ineffective. There are many Scriptures which convince without ambiguity that he is of another from all the conditions of nature. They are said to be: but no one, either in the Scriptures or in custom, is called a full creature. For neither does the Scripture claim this for itself, nor does common speech say that anyone is full of an angel, a throne, or dominion: since this speech belongs only to the divine nature. that some are full of virtue and discipline: as that, He is filled with the Holy Spirit (Exod. 31:3); signifying nothing else than that they are full of consummated and perfect virtue. another: And his father Zacharias was filled with the Holy Spirit (Ibid., 67). There is no doubt that John also prophesied. Isn't it written in the Acts of the Apostles about many believers who had come together as one: They were filled with the Holy Spirit (Acts 2, 4) But when the Holy Spirit is participable, like wisdom and discipline, it does not possess the substance of knowledge in the empty names: but through nature sanctifying and filling all things with good, the good itself subsists, according to which some are said to be filled with the Holy Spirit: as in the Acts of the Apostles it is written, And they were all filled with the Holy Spirit, and they spoke the word of God with confidence (Ibid.). For just as he who is full of any discipline, who has it perfectly, can speak about it with learning and precision, so those who have fully received the Holy Spirit, so that they may be filled with it, when they speak the word of God with confidence, because the present Holy Spirit ministers a voice worthy of God. And in many places of the Acts of the Apostles, it is written that the disciples of the Lord were full of the Holy Spirit. he was full of the Holy Spirit, looking up into heaven, he saw the glory of God, and Jesus standing at the right hand of God (Ibid., 5). 13, 9). And it is written in general about all believers: The disciples were also filled with joy and the Holy Spirit (Ibid., 52). But the presence of angels, or of any other excellent nature that has been made, does not fill the mind and sense: because and it is completed from another source. For just as from the fullness of one who receives the Savior, he is made full of wisdom, and power, and justice, and the word of God: so, he who is full of the Holy Spirit is immediately filled with all the gifts of God, wisdom, knowledge, faith, and other virtues. He fills all creatures, which, however, can receive power and wisdom, it is not from these things that He Himself completes. Finally, it is impossible for anyone to receive the grace of God if he does not have the Holy Spirit, in whom we approve that all the gifts of God consist of. We have said that the substance of God's goods is the Holy Spirit: when we set the example, the Father will give the Holy Spirit to those who ask him (Luke 11:13). And the Father will give good things to those who ask him (Matthew 5:11), to be divided, because it is called a multitude of goods. For it is impassive, and indivisible, and unchangeable; but according to different efficiency and understanding, he is called by many terms of good: because he does not give his participants according to one and the same virtue in his communion, since he is suited to the benefit of each one, and he fills with good those whom he judges that he ought to be present. Finally, Stephen is the first witness of the truth, and he was called worthy of his name full of wisdom and of the Holy Spirit: wisdom is consequently above the understanding, dwelling in him the Holy Spirit, as the Scripture says: And they chose Stephen full of faith, and the apostles with the Holy Spirit (Acts 6:5). but full of grace and power, he performed wonders and great signs among the people (Ibid., 8). blessed is the man, and he is a partaker of the effect of faith, which comes from the Holy Spirit, next to it, but others have faith in the same Spirit (1 Cor. 12:9). And having grace and power next to the same Spirit, he did great signs and wonders among the people. He did not also flow with those gifts according to the same Spirit, which are called healing graces and virtues. those who contradicted him, and those who argued against him, were able to resist the wisdom and the Spirit that spoke in him. For he was wise from the Holy Spirit. Whence Jesus clearly proclaims to his disciples: When you have been introduced to principalities, and powers, and councils, and synagogues, do not be anxious about what you ought to say, or what you will speak at that time. For you will be given by the Holy Spirit words of wisdom, with which they will not be able to contradict, not even those who are vehemently skilled in debates. But when they have brought you into the synagogues to the principalities and powers, do not worry about how or what you will answer, for the Holy Spirit will teach you in the same hour what to say (Matthew 12:12). , as you answer: For I will give you a mouth and wisdom, which they will not be able to contradict or answer (Luke 14:14). And how the Savior at that hour bestows mouth and wisdom on the disciples, whom they cannot contradict, even those who are thought to be the most eloquent among men, it is not for this time to argue; because we have now proposed to show that the superintelligent always have the gifts of virtue in the Holy Spirit; so that the one who has it may be considered full of God's gifts. Hence also in Isaiah, God himself says something: I will put my Spirit on your seed, and my blessings on your children (Isa. 44., 3). For no one ever receives spiritual blessings for he who has received the Holy Spirit will consequently have blessings, that is, wisdom, and understanding, and the rest, of which the apostle thus writes: For this reason, we also, from the day we heard, do not cease praying for you. and supplicating that you may be filled with the knowledge of his will in all wisdom and spiritual intelligence: walking worthy of God (Colossians 1:9). For those who are worthy of themselves through works, and words, and prudence, he says, to be filled with the will of God, who has placed upon them the Holy Spirit, that they may be filled with wisdom and understanding, and with other spiritual goods. But wisdom and understanding, which are in the Holy Spirit, are given by God. The Lord, he says, will give wisdom; and from his face proceeds wisdom and understanding (Ecclesiastes 1); with that wisdom which comes from men, let it not be spiritual, but carnal and human. Therefore, the Apostle writes about this: We were not in carnal wisdom, but in the grace of God in world (1 Cor. 1 and 2); speaking of carnal wisdom, which in corporeal things subsists from human thought. Furthermore, spiritual and intellectual wisdom, keeping itself around the invisible and intellectual, through the operation of the

Holy Spirit gives its presence to those who receive it. As in him: But may the God of hope fill you with all joy and peace in believing, that you may abound in hope and in the power of the Holy Spirit (Rom. 15:13). renders] in the power of the Holy Spirit, to those who have it; He fills with joy and peace those who, possessing an undisturbed and calm thought, have happy minds, and are calm from every storm of disturbances. He says the kingdom of God is not food and drink; but justice and peace and joy in the Holy Spirit (Rom. 14:17). For in the Holy Spirit, he proves most clearly that justice, that is, all power, and the peace which we have said above is coupled with the joy of God, to those who could hear him, these goods are not other than the substance of the Holy Spirit. Therefore, when these goods come to men from the bounty of the Holy Spirit, the calling of the Gentiles which he introduced through the teaching of the Gospel, is rendered acceptable and sanctified in the Holy Spirit: because both in this the Holy Spirit makes them sanctified and accepted , is the substance of the goods of God. , the bestowal of the Holy Spirit is the nature of the gifts of God. For he said to those who reproached his entrance to Cornelius: If then God gave equal grace to them by giving the Holy Spirit, how also to us in the beginning: who was I that could stop the Lord? And moreover, to his own, Acknowledgment, he says, the heart God bears witness to by giving them the Holy Spirit just as he did to us: and there was nothing between us and them, purifying their hearts by faith (Acts 15:8 seq.). This sense also corresponds to what is called the Spirit in many places. to be given holy by the Lord, my son Jacob, I will receive him: Israel my chosen, my soul will receive him: I have put my spirit in him (Isa. 42, 1). and the spirit of those who trample on it (Ibid, 5). We have shown above that there is no other Spirit of God, and another Holy Spirit. Paul also says, the charity of God has spread in your hearts, through the Holy Spirit who was given to you (Rom. 5:5). it is said that those who receive him may prophesy and see visions, according to Joel, who speaks from the person of God: I will pour out of my spirit upon all flesh: and your sons and your daughters will prophesy (Joel. 2, 28). For the outpouring of the spirit exists for a reason to prophesy, and to see the sense and beauty of truth. The very name of outpouring proves the uncreated substance of the Holy Spirit. This discourse agrees with those which are shared by others: just as we have now, and a little before, spoken of the charity of God, which is shed abroad in the hearts of those who have received the Holy Spirit. for you (Rom. 5:5). The Savior also, because he himself is capable, is also said to be poured out in the likeness of ointment: Thy name is poured out with ointment (Cant. 1:2).

THE HOLY GHOST

but it is forbidden to spread farther, because the inner vessel is closed: but when the vessel has been poured out, it emits its sweetness far away: thus, the sweet-smelling name of Christ, before his coming, was surrounded only by the people of Israel, as if it were enclosed in a vessel of Judea. For God is known, he says, in Judea, his name is great in Israel (Psal. 75, 2). And when the Savior, shining in his flesh, extended his name to the whole earth, rather than to every creature, fulfilling what is written: How Your name is wonderful in all the earth (Psal. VIII, 2, 10); to whom the Apostle speaks in consequence: For there is no other name given under heaven in which it is necessary to be saved (Act. 4, 12): and the Psalmist speaks to the Lord, thou hast magnified thy holy name above all things: then it is complete, thy name poured out with ointment. When one person somewhere, or two receive the Holy Spirit, it is not said that the Spirit will be poured out, but then when the gift of the Holy Spirit has overflowed into all nations. regeneration and renewal of the Holy Spirit, whom He pours out upon us abundantly (Titus 3:5), which is captured by many, and gives them its own company: but that which is capable is that which is filled by the communication of the substance of another: and grasping something else, it itself is not grasped from another. For the capable is immediately inconvertible, and the inconvertible is eternally consequent: just as, on the contrary, the convertible is convertible to the convertible, and the convertible is subsequent to the creative. Therefore, nothing of creatures is inconvertible, for which reason it is not eternal. Therefore, not only that which is rational in men is converted, and is created, but this same conversion is found in all creatures. It is clearly shown that in the first state they continue not by the immutability of their substance, but by a more anxious service in the Lord. to the superiors they are immortal, there is no doubt that all things constituted in the same kind and species are immortal. bodies are divisible, though not all are divisible. For some of their divisions interpret the nature of the division, and of the rest of their kind. holy: saying that in the fact that all things were made by God through the Word, the work of the Holy Spirit is also signified. corporeal and incorporeal: and the Holy Spirit is created, of course, he will be either a visible or an invisible creature, that is, corporeal or incorporeal. A true body will never be, as we said before, when it teaches, and provides knowledge, and is seized by sense and soul but neither will he be an invisible creature, as we discussed a little earlier about him. Whence the Apostle in the Epistle which he wrote to the Hebrews shows that he is different from all the angels, saying: For to whom he once said to the angels: Sit at my right hand, until I make your enemies a stool your feet? Are not all stewards of the spirit, sent into ministry, for those who were about to receive salvation (Hebrews 1, 13)? And after another: How shall we escape, neglecting so much salvation? heard it confirmed in us, bearing witness to God with signs, and wonders, and various powers, and the divisions of the Holy Spirit according to his will (Hebrews 2:4). an angelic name signifying the substance of all invisible creatures. For God did not say to any of the angels, nor to any other reasonable creature: Sit at my right hand. Therefore, he utters a common speech, that it should not be said to any of the creatures, Sit at my right hand. And this is in common about creatures and speaking of all invisible creatures, he says that they are administrators of spirits. Because of what he submitted: Are not all administrators of spirits sent to serve? They are the very possibility of the masses: the consorts of the masses and equal substances. How then is the Lord different from all creatures, through whom he received the principle to speak that great salvation, whose neglect the apostle did not want us to be, says: How shall we escape by neglecting so much salvation, which receiving the principle to speak by the Lord, it was confirmed in us by those who heard; but God, who bears witness to these signs and portents of salvation, is different from all administrative spirits; so also the Holy Spirit, by whose divisions God bears witness according to his will, distributing him, not by the parts of circumcision, but by the communion with whom he has decided to give him: he is also of another's substance from these, into which he is divided. sense, that the Holy Spirit is another outside of all creation, when they want to show that some have been created unfailingly, indeed impiously, they make use of the testimony by which all things done by the Word are related: namely, that in all things also the eternal substance is contained. , saying to God, I create a spirit: even in this we must point out that they are completely alien to the understanding of the truth. Nor was the speech of the Prophet proposed about the Holy Spirit, as is understood from the very series and context of the speech. let us call upon your God, O Israel: for I am the one who strengthens the thunder, and creates the spirit, and announces to men his Christ: making the dawn and the mist and ascending above the heights of the earth: the Lord God Almighty is his name (Amos 4:13). He had foretold to establish the spirit, and to make it: and he said to establish the thunder, and to make the dawn and the clouds. Let it be like this to God: That you may call upon me, who am God, who procures all things, who am also the creator of all, who makes the thunder, and carries the spirit, who makes the dawn and the cloud for certain interests of men: to prepare, that you may call, O Israel: that when be prepared to invoke, and pray to me, who appoints the aforesaid, that you may enjoy the happiness of the seasons and the bounties of other goods, that I may serve you every year according to the order of nature, that the year may flow fruitfully, that the moments of the hours may run through their spaces, that the thunders may roar in their season , so that the salutary breeze may inspire with suitable blasts. If, however, the allegory, the thunder and the dawn, and the fog, and the creation of the spirit, are understood, they will not signify the substance of the thing, but a figurative interpretation.

15. But if he opposed from a different point of view that these things should be said of the Holy Spirit, because he is brought to the creation of the Spirit, what follows: And proclaiming his Christ to all men (Ibid.); It is found in the Hebrew, he declares his speech in man; that is to say, he who is the creator of all, himself also of the prophets, and through them he will reveal his will to men. firming] the thunder, and creating the spirit, and making and governing other parts of the world, announcing to men my Christ. Humility belongs to the existing cause. I think that what is said, I create the spirit, is just as well placed, as if it were said, creating the wind. For God the breath, which is made by the movement of the air, leads by his disposition: according to what we read elsewhere: He who produces the winds of his treasures (Psal. 134, 7). But it is good that in the sentence itself he does not say, I created: but he who creates the spirit. For if the word were about the substantiality of the Holy Spirit, he would certainly have said, he who created. For he does not always create the same person. Now and in consequence it is said of the breath that I create: for the winds were not once made, but in that which they subsist, they are made daily. since the Holy Spirit is almost always named with an article, as in that αὐτὸ τὸ Πνεῦμα, that is, the Spirit himself bears witness to our spirit (Rom. VIII, 16). It is possible to extract many things from the sacred Scriptures. Although the Holy Spirit is rarely mentioned without an article, it must be known that he is mentioned with an addition signifying his magnificence. Helias, and walk in the Spirit (4 Kings 2, 15; Galatians 5, 16), and whatever are similar to these.

16. Since, therefore, from these things which I have mentioned, and from many others, it has been shown that the Holy Spirit is not a creature, he is never numbered with conditions, but is always placed with the Father and the Son:

now let us see how indifferent he is to both. At the end of the second Epistle, which Paul writes to the Corinthians, he says: May the grace of our Lord Jesus Christ, and the charity of God, and the communion of the Holy Spirit be always with you all (II Cor. xiii, 13). one assumption of the Trinity: since he who has received the grace of Christ, has it both through the administration of the Father and through the bestowal of the Holy Spirit. For it is given by God the Father and Jesus Christ, according to that: Grace be with you, and peace from God the Father, and the Lord Jesus Christ (Rom. 1, 7; 1 Cor. 1, 3; Coloss. 1, et al.): not giving another grace to the Father and the other Savior. Indeed, he describes it as being given by the Father and the Lord Jesus Christ, completed by the communication of the Holy Spirit. For the Spirit himself is said to be grace, according to the saying: And doing injury to the spirit of grace, in which he was sanctified (Heb. 10:29). Jerusalem the spirit of grace and mercy (Zechar. 12, 10). For when anyone receives the grace of the Holy Spirit, he will have it given by God the Father and by Jesus Christ our Lord. One grace, therefore, completed by the operation of the Father and the Son and the Holy Spirit, the Trinity is shown of one substance. In another place also, he says (2 Cor. xiii, 13), the charity of God is with you all, which is both given and established by the Trinity. He loves me. But he who loves me will be loved by my Father, and I will love him (John 14:21). For there is no other love of the Savior for those who love him, and another love of the Father. For God loves unto salvation, because so God so loved the world, that he gave his only begotten Son: that whosoever believeth in him [the Son] should not perish but have eternal life (John 3:16). Similarly, the Son, who is life, may give life and salvation, he loves those whom he wants to become better. Hence, he says that he loves him who is loved by the Father.

17. That this love is the fruit of the Holy Spirit, the Apostle contends, as well as joy and peace, which are ministered by the Father and the Son, saying: But the fruit of the Spirit is joy, peace, charity (Galatians 5, 22). What charity has been poured out in the hearts of believers by the Holy Spirit. Indeed, he says, the charity of God has been poured out in your hearts in the Holy Spirit (Rom. 5:5). by his participation he shares, according to that. And let the communion of the Holy Spirit always be with you all (II Cor. xiii, 13). And in another place: If any communion of the Spirit. a partnership of holiness in the Father, and in the Son, and in the Holy Spirit. But God is faithful, through whom you were

called into the fellowship of his Son (1 Cor. 1, 9). John also writes about the Father: If we walk in the light, as he is in the light, we have communion with him (1 John 1:7). And again: Our communion is with the Father and his Son Jesus Christ. contributed by the Holy Spirit. But he who is a partaker of the grace of Jesus Christ has the same grace, given by the Father through the Holy Spirit. substance: because those which are of the same substance have the same operations; and those which are of another substance, and ἀνομούσια, are discordant and different. We will put a few things in order. yours, that you would lie to the Holy Spirit and hide the price of the land? Did the remaining one not remain with you, and the sale was in your power? Why did you put this matter in your heart? For if he who lies to the Lord lies to the Holy Spirit, and he who lies to the Holy Spirit lies to God, there is no doubt that the Holy Spirit has fellowship with God. divinity] is meant in the Holy Spirit. Now this Holy Spirit, whom we have said is of the same nature with the Father, does not differ from the divinity of the Son, as the Savior said to the disciples: When they have brought you into the Synagogue to principalities and powers, do not worry how or what you will answer For the Holy Spirit will teach you at that hour what you ought to say. Put it in your hearts not to premeditate to answer. indeed, saying that they ought not to be anxious what they should answer to those who contradict, because in the same hour they are taught by the Holy Spirit what they ought to answer. wisdom, which they will not be able to resist or contradict (Luke 21:14). For when he says, in the time of answering, they will be taught by the Holy Spirit what they should answer, he says in what follows: For I will give you mouth and wisdom, etc.

19. By which it is shown that the wisdom which is given to the disciples by the Son of the Holy Spirit is wisdom: and the teaching of the Holy Spirit is the teaching of the Lord: and that the partnership of the Holy Spirit with the Son is one in nature and will. But the Son and the Father are one, according to that: I and the Father are one (John 10:30): not divided and inseparable, according to nature, the Trinity is shown. In another Gospel it is also said: For it is not you who speak, but the Spirit of your Father who speaks in you (Matthew 10:20). If then the Spirit of the Father speaks in the apostles, teaching those who ought to answer and what is taught by the Spirit is wisdom, which we cannot understand other than the Son: it clearly appears that the Spirit is of the same nature with the Son, and with the Father, whose Spirit he is.

20. Through another example of the Scriptures, the unity and nature and power of the Trinity is shown. The Son is called the hand, the right hand, and the arm of the Father. The Holy Spirit is also named, the finger of God, according to the conjunction of the nature of the Father and the Son. Indeed, in one of the Gospels against those who took away the signs of the Lord, saying: In Beelzebub, the prince of the demons, he casts out the demons (Matthew 9:34). If I cast out demons in Beelzebub, where do your children cast them out? And if I cast out demons in the finger of God, then the kingdom of God has come upon you (Luke 11:19). but I cast out demons in the Spirit of God. By which it is shown that the finger of God is the Holy Spirit. cast low, and forgetting the conversation about which we are now debating, picture in your mind the diversities of the bodily limbs; , to disagree with many inequalities: because the Scripture now speaks of incorporeal things, wanting only to show unity, not even to show the measure of substance: for just as the hand is not divided from the body, through which it accomplishes and works everything, and is in that, whose hand it is: so neither is the finger it is separated from the hand, whose finger it is. So, reject inequalities and measures, when you think of God, and understand the unity of the finger and the hand, and of the whole substance: with which finger the law was written on tablets of stone. Through another Scripture, it is very easy to show the proof of our faith Only God is said to be wise: he is not called wise by receiving wisdom from another, nor by any part of the wisdom of another. He alone is said to be wise, and begetting wisdom, and making others wise. What wisdom is the Lord our Jesus Christ, who is called the power of God, and the wisdom of God. The Holy Spirit is also called wisdom. just as God alone is wise, not receiving wisdom from elsewhere, but making wise men and generating wisdom: he alone is wise, apart from all those who are called wise by his name: for the multitude of wise men is the salvation of the world (Wisdom 6:26): they know themselves, these are the wise: And again: When you are with the wise, you will be wise (Prov. 13:20): so also the Holy Spirit, not receiving wisdom from another, is called the spirit of wisdom: for this very thing that subsists is the spirit of wisdom: and his nature is nothing else but the Spirit of truth and the Spirit of God: about which we have already discussed abundantly in the volume of Sectaries. So that we do not repeat the same things unnecessarily, let us be content with the past discussion. and truth. For if he were capable of wisdom and truth, he would sometimes descend into it, so that he would cease to have what he had received from elsewhere: that is, wisdom and truth. is predicated. We see that the same circle

of unity and substance of the Holy Spirit, according to what is the spirit of wisdom and truth, we see with the Son: and again, the Son does not differ in substance from the Father. But since the Son is the image of the invisible God, and the form of the substance of him, whosoever are imagined to this image, or form, and are formed into the likeness of God: yet, proceeding according to the powers of man, they follow the form and image of that kind. him, in him they are led to the sign of Christ's wisdom and knowledge, full of faith. by the Holy Spirit. For others the word of wisdom is given by the Spirit. To others, knowledge, according to the same Spirit. To others, faith in the same Spirit, and the rest of the gifts which are enumerated by the Apostle, to which is added: But all these things work one and the same Spirit: dividing to each one as he wills (Ibid., 8 seq.).

23. Whence they say the active, and so to speak, distributive nature of the Holy Spirit: let us not be led astray by those who say that the Holy Spirit is the operation and not the substance of God. And from many other places as well the subsisting nature of the Holy Spirit is shown, as in what the apostles write: "For it was seen by the Holy Spirit and by us" (Acts 15:28). should be found, that: As it pleased the Lord, so it was done (Job.1). Finally, his words are read very often, as in that: To those who fasted and ministered to them: that is, to the disciples of Christ, the Holy Spirit said: Separate Barnabas and Saul for me. to the work to which I called them (Acts 13:2). Which voice of divinity and authority indicates not a created, but an uncreated substance. For the Holy Spirit did not call Barnabas and Paul to any other work, which is not that of the Father and the Son: when the ministry which he committed and delivered to them should be the ministry of the Spirit, of the Father and of the Son. Paul is speaking to the Galatians. they were directed by the authority of the saints. In Christ also working in the apostles, the Spirit is a complete ministry, so that the apostles themselves confess that they speak in Christ, and what they saw with their own eyes, and they became ministers of the word, that is, of Christ: and stewards of the mysteries of God. possessing the leadership in the priesthood, and the initiators of the faith were pointed out by Christ, saying: Go and teach all the nations, baptizing them in the name of the Father, and of the Son, and of the Holy Spirit (Matthew 28:19). And as the Apostle writes most correctly: One is the Lord, one faith, one baptism. Who is not compelled by the truth itself to accept the indifference of the Holy Trinity, while there is one faith in

the Father, and the Son, and the Holy Spirit: and the washing is given and confirmed in the name of the Father, and of the Son, and of the Holy Spirit?

24. I do not think that anyone will be so vexatious and insane as to think that baptism is perfect if it is given in the name of the Father and of the Son, without the assumption of the Holy Spirit; holy, not by the word Father. He will not be able to deliver from the sins of those whom he thought he had baptized. From these it is gathered that the substance of the Trinity is undivided, and that the Father is truly the Father of the Son, and the Son is truly the Son of the Father: and the Holy Spirit is truly the Spirit of the Father and of God; that is, the children of God. This, then, is the salvation of believers, and the dispensation of ecclesiastical discipline is completed in this Trinity., on this matter also the apostle's consistent sentence: And as we have been tested by God to believe the Gospel, so we speak: not to please men, but to God who tested our hearts (1 Thess. 2, 4): these same ones whom Christ commanded to be teachers, and the Father approved, and the Holy Spirit is said to have appointed stewards and superiors in the Church. Indeed, when in Miletus the apostle Paul had gathered the priests from different places and many churches: Pay attention, he said, to yourselves and to the whole flock, over whom the Holy Spirit has appointed you bishops to govern the Church of the Lord, which he acquired through his blood (Acts 20:28)? For if those whom Christ sent to evangelize and baptize the nations, the Holy Spirit placed them before the Church, destined by the will of the Father: there is no doubt that the Father, and the Son, and the Holy Spirit are one operation and proof: and consequently, that the same is the substance of the Trinity. to be considered, that no creature can dwell in the heart and sense, except God and his word in the Holy Spirit: just as the Father says to some: I will dwell in them and walk in them (II Cor. 6, 16). And someone directs his voice to him: You but you dwell in the holy, praise Israel (Psal. XXI, 4). For the founder of all creation dwells high in the high. Indeed, the only begotten Son also dwells in the pure mind and heart of those who believe. For by faith Christ dwells in the inner man: in the Spirit he says the apostle, writing thus: In the Spirit, in the inner man, Christ may dwell in your hearts through faith (Ephesians 3:17). He also speaks of himself: Christ lives in me (Galatians 2:20). And again: He who lives in me Christ speaks (2 Cor. xiii, 3). And the Savior, we will come, he says, I and the Father (John xiv. 23): no doubt, but to him who has kept his precepts, and we

THE HOLY GHOST

will make our abode with him. It is connected: If anyone loves me, he will keep my word. And my Father will love him, and we will come to him and make our abode with him (Ibid.). In another place also, the whole nature of rational creatures is called the house of the Savior. over his house the Lord Jesus, whose house we are: so, the house of Christ is the temple of God, in which the same Spirit of God dwells. For Paul, writing to the Corinthians, says: Do you not know that you are the temple of God, and the Spirit of God dwells in you (1 Cor. 3, 16)? But if in the house and temple where the Father and the Savior dwell, the Holy Spirit is also found there, from this the undivided substance of the Trinity is shown. God (ibid.)? When then the Holy Spirit, in the same way as the Father and the Son, is taught to inhabit the mind and the inner man, I do not call him foolish, but it is impious to call him a creature, and it is possible for affections to dwell in souls: not, however, as substantives, but as accidents. But it is impossible for created nature to dwell in sense. That if it be true, and the Holy Spirit subsisting without any ambiguity, is the inhabitant of the soul and of the heart: there is no doubt, for the uncreated must be believed with the Father and the Son. Therefore, from all that is discussed in the preceding discourse, the Holy Spirit, shown to be incorruptible and eternal according to the nature of the Father and the Son, removed from himself all ambiguity and suspicion, lest he should be considered one of the created substances. , that he is the Spirit of God, whom the words of the Savior declare in the Gospel to proceed from the Father. When he comes, he says, the Comforter, whom I will send to you, the Spirit of truth, who proceeds from the Father, he himself will testify about me (John 15:26). but he speaks of the coming of the Holy Spirit, giving him a name from his operation: because he not only consoles those whom he has found worthy, and delivers strangers from all sadness and confusion; such a guest should be considered worthy, to say: You have given joy in my heart (Psal. 4, 7). For eternal joy dwells in the hearts of those whose Holy Spirit is the indweller. the ministry of the apostles, but that the Spirit of God should be sent by wisdom and truth, having an indivisible nature with the same wisdom and truth. The Son proceeds from the Father, not transmigrating from one place to another. For this is both impossible and blasphemous. To believe what we have said about the incorporeal: that the Holy Spirit proceeds from the Father, is to be understood in this way, that the Savior testifies that he proceeded from God, saying, "I proceeded from God and came" (John 8:42). Thus, we distinguish the utterances within the speaker and without the nature of intellectuals, because these are the bodies of those who receive the touch, and the wastes of those who have them. for when he could speak of God, or of the Lord, or of the Almighty, he touched none of these: but he says, of the Father: not that the Father is different from God the Almighty: for this is also a crime to think; but according to the propriety and understanding of the parent, the Spirit of truth is said to proceed from him. To the Father, and the Father in me (John 14:10). And elsewhere: I and the Father are one (John 10:30) it goes out, it will be witnessed; says the Lord, about me, bearing witness to him similar to the testimony of the Father, of which he says: He testifies about me that the Father sent me (John 12:49). for the Father sending the Son does not send, but the Spirit comes with the same will of the Father and the Son. The Savior also spoke through the Prophet: as will be evident to him who has read the whole place. God sends. But the apostle also speaks: What has now been announced to you by those who preached the gospel to you, sent by the Holy Spirit from heaven (1 Pet. 1, 12). But who has searched out what is in the heavens? But who has known your will? Except that you have given wisdom and sent your Holy Spirit from on high? men (Wisdom 9:17). And in the present reading, not only the wisdom of God, that is, his only-begotten Son, is given by the Father, but also the Holy Spirit is sent. Saint, the Savior saying: And I will ask my Father, and he will give you another Paraclete, that he may be with you forever, the spirit of truth (John XIV, 16). And again, the Paraclete is the Holy Spirit, whom the Father will send in my name: he you he will teach all things (Ibid., 26). For even in these words, the Father is said to give another paraclete, but not another from him who is sent by the Son according to the saying: "But when that paraclete comes, whom I will send to you from the Father, the Spirit of truth" (John 15:26). , let him have the person of a mediator and ambassador, and with whom the pontiff is implored for our sins, saving forever those who have come to God through him, because the ever-living intercedes for them to the Father; The Holy Spirit, according to another significance, is called a paraclete, from that which comforts those in sorrow. Do not, indeed, esteem different natures from the operation of the Son and the Holy Spirit. For in another place the paraclete Spirit is found, acting as the person of the ambassador to the Father, as in him: For we do not know what we should pray, but the Spirit himself intercedes for us with indescribable groans. when] according to God he asks for the saints (Rom. VIII, 26). 28. The Savior also works the consolation by which the Holy Spirit was called the paraclete, in the hearts of those who need it. For it is written: And he comforted the lowly people (Ps. 32). Whence also to those who had obtained this benefit, preaching it, he spoke: Lord, according to the multitude of my sorrows in my heart, your consolations have made my heart happy (Psal. 203, 19); or they loved my soul: for it is written in both ways, it is found in different copies. therefore, the comforting and holy Spirit, and the Spirit of truth, is given by the Father, that he may always dwell with Christ's disciples, with whom he is also the Savior, saying: For behold, I am with you until the end of the age (Matthew 28:20). to the apostles and the Holy Spirit and the Son, it follows that the Father is also with them, because he who receives the Son receives the Father also: and the Son makes his abode with the Father among those who have existed worthy of his coming. Since the Holy Spirit is in the prophets, causing them to foretell the future, and other things of prophetic activity, the word of God is said to have been made to them, so that to what is customary for the prophets, these things says the Lord, let that also be added, the word that was made to Isaiah, or to the rest.

29. But we know that the prophets had the Holy Spirit, speaking clearly to God. They had announced his coming to the people, filled with the aspiration of the Holy Spirit. For when he asked the Pharisees what they saw of Christ, and hearing that he was the son of David, he says: How does David in the Spirit call him Lord, saying: The Lord said to my Lord, sit at my right hand? If then David calls him in the Holy Spirit the Lord, how is his Son (Matthew 22:43)? And Peter speaks to the companions of the faith: It was necessary to fulfill the Scripture, which the Holy Spirit foretold through the mouth of David of Judah, etc. (Acts 1, 16). Again, in the same book: Who through the Spirit, says he, spoke through the holy mouth of David thy son: Why did the nations roar, and the people meditated in vain (Act. iv, 25)? As is written at the end of the same Acts. Well, the Holy Spirit spoke through the prophet Isaiah to your fathers, saying: Go to this people and say: You will hear with your ears, and the rest (Acts 28:25). Therefore, this prophecy which the Apostle Paul affirms is spoken by the Holy Spirit, the same book of the prophets mentions that it was spoken by the Lord. And I heard, says Isaiah, the voice of the Lord, saying: Whom shall I send, and who will go to these people? And I said: Behold, I am, send me. To these people: You will hear with your ears (Isa. 6:9). And after another the Lord himself said: And they will be converted, and I will heal them. And immediately the prophet: How long, Lord? and the Prophet replied to the commanding Lord, 'How long, Lord?' by the nomenclature of the Spirit is also

to be understood the name of the Lord. For just as to the Corinthians the term of God is placed above the Father, and of the Lord above the Son, it does not take away the dominion of the Father, nor the deity of the Son. And if the Lord, consequently also God: as we said a little before, when we put the voice of the Apostle Peter to Ananias, who had stolen the money: because divinity is super intelligible in the Holy Spirit, if we can find anything in it to agree with what has been said. In which appellation of the Son, the Holy Spirit, sent by the Father, is understood, not a servant, not another, and not separated from the Son. And how the Son comes at the Father's appeal, saying: I have come in the name of my Father (John 5:43): for the Son can only come in the name of the Father, save the propriety of the Son to the Father, and of the Father to the Son: so on the contrary, no one else comes in the name of the Father, but for example, in the name of the Lord, and of God, and of the Almighty. Which you will be able to notice clearly by reading the prophets from your heart. For even Moses is a great minister and servant of God, in the name of him who is: Abraham and Isaac, and Jacob came, God speaking to him: Thus, you shall say to the children of Israel, who is, sent me to you (Exodus 3:15). And again, you shall say to them, God sent Abraham, Isaac, and Jacob to you. For the righteous servants were such as those about whom he said: I will command my servants the prophets in my Spirit (Zech. 1:6), the mission was made in the name of God. And because who showed themselves worthy of God, are reported to have come in the name of God. Again, progressing to a greater place, and being consistent under the rule of one God, they came in the name of the Almighty God. But since the children of Israel were living in Egypt, they learned to worship those who are not, as if they were gods. and the fathers of the world were to be venerated with divine honor: the consequence was that Moses was sent to them under the name of his, who is, and, delivering them from the falsities of the gods, converted them to the true deity, and to the Lord, the father of Abraham, Isaac, and Jacob. 31. How therefore the servants who come in the name of the Lord, by the very fact that they are subject and serve, indicate the Lord, referring to his property: since they are the servants of the Lord: so also the Son who comes in the name of the Father, bears the property of the Father and the name, and by this the only begotten The Son of God is approved. Since then, the Holy Spirit is sent by the Father in the name of the Son, having the property of the Son, according as he is God, yet not the sonship, so that he is his Son, he shows that he is joined to the Son in unity. Whence also the Spirit is called the Son, making by adoption children, those who wanted to receive themselves. For whom, says he, are the children of God, the Father sent the Spirit of his Son into our hearts, crying Abba Father (Rom. 8, 15). And this Holy Spirit, who comes in the name of the Son, sent by to the father: he will teach all things to those who are perfect in the faith of Christ. But all those things which are spiritual and intellectual: and to briefly conclude all, all the sacraments of truth and wisdom. This belongs to those who learn wisdom and certain arts by study and energy; but as if the art and doctrine and wisdom and truth of the Spirit, invisibly to the mind insinuates the knowledge of the divine. For the father also teaches his disciples in this way, saying to him who had been taught by him: God, you have taught me wisdom. And in this way all become learned. The Son of God and the wisdom of God and the truth thus teach their fellows, so that discipline is not taught by art, but by nature. Whence also the disciples are taught to call him only teacher. The Holy Spirit ministers to those who have ceased to be animals. For man, being an animal, does not perceive those things which are spirits; judging that what is said is foolishness (1 Cor. 2:14); But he who has cleansed his mind from distractions will be filled with the teachings of the Holy Spirit, that is, with the words of wisdom and knowledge: to the extent that he who has received them says: God has revealed himself to us through the Holy Spirit (Ibid., 10). they have prepared the Spirit of wisdom and revelation is given to know oneself: those who receive the Spirit of wisdom, not from another place, but from the Holy Spirit Himself, are made wise, and from Him they understand the Lord and whatever is of God's will, and they know the same Spirit Himself, revealing Him, so that they may know that they were given to them by the Lord: so that he who has obtained the spirit of revelation and wisdom is sufficient to preach the doctrines of truth, not human, but supported by the art of God. in the words of human wisdom: but in the manifestation of the Spirit and the power of God (Ibid., 4). But we cannot interpret a power equal to the Spirit other than Christ our Lord. And to Mary, the Angel, the Holy Spirit, he says, will come upon you, and the power of the Most High will overshadow you (Luke 1:35). Therefore, the creator, the power of the Most High, by the Holy Spirit coming into the virgin Mary, made the body of Christ: which he used in the temple, he was born without a husband seed.

32. From which it is shown that the Holy Spirit is the creator, as we have already shown briefly in the volume of Dogmata. you will renew the face of the

THE HOLY GHOST

earth (Psal. 13:30). Nor is it surprising if the Holy Spirit is the creator of Dominic's body alone, joined with the Father and the Son, and created with the same power all that the Father and the Son created. For send forth, he says, your Spirit, and they will be created. We have frequently shown that the Holy Spirit is of the same operation, of whom the Father and the Son are, and that in the same operation there is one substance, in the Gospel the word is woven together like this: I still have many things to say to you, but you cannot bear them alone. But when that Spirit of truth comes, he will direct you to all truth. He will glorify me: because he will receive of mine, and will declare it to you. , that when Jesus had taught many things to his disciples, he said: I still have many things to say to you, because this word, I still have many things to say to you, is not directed to any new ones, and completely empty of the grace of God: but to those who are hearers of his words, and have not yet had all For whatever they were able to suffice, he handed over to them the rest for a future time, which they could not know without the instruction of the Holy Spirit: because before the coming of Sunday's Passion the Holy Spirit had not been given to men, the Evangelist saying: For the Spirit had not been given to anyone, because Jesus had not yet He was glorified (John 7:39). He was glorified, saying that Jesus would taste death for all. Thus, after the resurrection, he appeared to his disciples and breathed into their faces: Receive, he said, the Holy Spirit (John 20:22). And again: You will receive the power of the Holy Spirit coming upon you (Acts 1:8). When it comes into the hearts of those who believe, they are filled with words of wisdom and knowledge, and thus spiritually effected, they receive the discipline of the Holy Spirit, which can lead them into all truth.] the hour in which it was necessary for them to be filled with the Holy Spirit, then when he said to them, I still have many things to say to you, he added consequently, but you cannot carry them alone (John 16:12). , they could not look at the truth (the shadow of which the law carried), and therefore they could not endure spiritual things. the life-giving spirit, in which alone all the truth of the Scriptures is placed. The Spirit of truth himself, entering a pure and simple mind, will seal in you the knowledge of truth, and always adding the new to the old, will direct you into all truth.

34. Some also alleging prayers to God the Father, says: Guide me in your truth (Psal. XXIV, 5): this is, in your Only Begotten, testifying with his own voice: I am the truth (John. XIV, 6). direct the truth. Henceforth, in the consequences

of the Spirit of truth, who is sent by the Father, and is a paraclete, the Savior (who is also truth) says: For he will not speak of himself (John 16:13): that is, not without me, and without mine and the will of the Father, because it is inseparable from mine and the Father's will. Because it is not from itself, but from the Father and me, for this very thing that stands and speaks is from the Father and me to him. I speak the truth, that is, I inspire what for it is the Spirit of truth. But to say and to speak in the Trinity is not to be accepted according to our custom, by which we talk and speak to each other, but according to the form of the incorporeal natures, and especially of the Trinity, which implants its will in the hearts of those who believe, and of those who they are worthy to hear it! that is, to say and to speak. Just as we strike the tongue with the palate and the teeth, and adjust the blow of the air into different words, so that we may communicate to others what is known to us, so also it is necessary for the hearer to provide open ears, and with no fault restricted, to what is said to establish, so that he may know what is uttered in the same way as he who speaks knows them. Further, God is of a simple and uncompounded spiritual nature, having neither ears nor organs by which the voice is emitted; but the isolated and incomprehensible substance is composed of no members and parts. Which indeed must be taken in the same way from the Son and from the Holy Spirit. Gen. 1, 3), and if anything, similar to these, worthy we must accept of God. For the Father does not declare his will to the Son (who is wisdom and truth) without being ignorant, since all that he speaks, wise and subsisting in truth, has wisdom and substance. To hear the Father speaking to the Son is the signification of the same nature and consent in the Father and the Son. The Holy Spirit, too, who is the spirit of truth and the spirit of wisdom, cannot hear what the Son does not know when speaking to the Son, since this is the very thing that is brought forth by the Son, that is, proceeding from truth, the comforter flowing from the comforter, God from God, the Spirit of truth proceeding. Finally, lest anyone should distinguish him from the will and association of the Father and the Son, it is written: For he will not speak of himself, but as he hears, he will speak (John 16:13). To whom also the Savior says of himself: As I hear, and I judge (John 5:30). , not according to Sabellius, who confounds the Father and the Son, but according to the indiscernibility of the essence, or substance, he cannot do anything without the Father, because the works of the separated are different, but seeing the Father working, he also works, not in a second degree and working after him. since the works of the Father and the Son would begin to be different, if they were not done equally.

by the same time of working the same and unlike things, all things that are made stand, and the Son cannot do anything by himself, because he cannot be separated from the Father, so also the Holy Spirit, being in no way separated from the Son, because of the union of his will and nature, is not believed to speak by himself, but according to Everything that speaks the word and truth of God. The following words of the Lord confirm this opinion, saying: He will glorify me, that is, the Paraclete, because he will receive from me. Again here, to receive, that it should be understood according to the divine nature. for] that which he gives, he does not impart to others with his loss, so also the Spirit does not receive what he did not have before. another] in the function of the empty giver is the result, ceasing to have what he gives. Therefore, just as we understood above when discussing incorporeal natures, so also now to receive the Holy Spirit from the Son, that which was to be known of his own nature, and not as giving and receiving, but as signifying one substance. For the Son also is said to receive from the Father those things by which he himself subsists. that which is given to him by the Son. Now these things are said to be proper, so that we may believe that in the Trinity it is the same nature of the Holy Spirit, which is the nature of the Father and the Son.

38. Because then every human voice can judge nothing else than bodies, and the Trinity, of which we are now speaking, surpasses all material substances, therefore no word can properly be appropriated to it, and signify its substance, but everything that we speak, καταχρηστικῶς, that is, it is abusive, and of all incorporeal things, and especially when we speak of the Trinity. Therefore, the Holy Spirit glorifies the Son, showing him and bringing him forth into the open to those who are worthy to understand and see him with a pure heart, and to know the splendor of the substance, and the image of the invisible God. Showing herself with pure minds, she glorifies the Father, insinuating him to those who do not know, for he himself says: He who sees me, sees the Father also (John 14:9). magnificence and power. But the Son himself, giving the Holy Spirit to those who have prepared themselves worthy of his office, and spreading his sublimity of glorification, and the power of his greatness, he glorifies him. Then, bringing the interpretation when he had just said, he will receive from me, he directly submitted. All that the Father has, are mine; that is why I said, he will receive of mine and will announce it to you (John 16:14), speaking in a certain way, Although the Spirit of truth proceeds from the

Father, and God gives him the Holy Spirit to those who ask him, nevertheless, because all that the Father has is mine, and he is the Spirit of the Father he is mine, and he will receive of mine. But when these things are said, beware lest you slip into a vice of heavy intelligence, and think that there is something, and possession, which is held by the Father and the Son. incorruption, unchangeable goodness, subsisting in himself and in himself, the same things the Son has. They are driven away, and seizing the opportunity of impiety from pious preaching, saying: Therefore, the Father is the Son, and the Son the Father. the things that my Father has are mine, he declared himself the Son in the name of the Father, he did not usurp the paternity which was the Son: although he himself, through the grace of adoption, is the Father of many saints, according to what is read in the Psalms, if your children keep. And again, if his children forsake my law (Psal. 88:31). But in this discourse and in the sense above, consequently, what we said is above the Father, the Son also has, and the Holy Spirit also has what the Sons are, he will receive from me, therefore he will announce to you what is to come. Indeed, through the Spirit of truth, holy men are granted a certain knowledge of the future. Whence also the prophets, filled with this same Spirit, foretold with sense, and looked as if they were present, what were to follow. it is sufficient to have said poverty in the present chapter of the Gospel. But if those to whom the Lord has revealed, and are brought into the neighborhood of the truth, and are more able to see the truth, let us grant better things to their discussion, supported by him who is the Spirit of truth. and diligently they grant forgiveness, to those who desire to offer all that they could to God, even though they did not want to fulfill their own will. who do not walk according to the flesh, but according to the Spirit. For those who are according to the flesh understand the things of the flesh. But those who follow the Spirit understand the things of the spirit. For the wisdom of the flesh is death. it is hostile to God: for it is not subject to the law of God. For neither can it. But those who are in the flesh cannot please God. But you are not in the flesh, but in the Spirit: if the Spirit of God dwells in you. But if Christ is in you, the body is dead because of sin, but the spirit lives because of righteousness. But if the Spirit of him who raised Jesus from the dead lives in you, he who raised Jesus Christ from the dead will give life your mortal bodies because of his indwelling Spirit in you. Therefore, brothers, we are debtors not to the flesh, that we may live according to the flesh. For if you live according to the flesh, you will die. But if by the spirit you have mortified the deeds of the flesh, you will live. He tells our spirit that we are children of God. But if we are

THE HOLY GHOST

indeed children and heirs of God, then we are co-heirs with Christ: if we have compassion, let us also be glorified (Rom. VIII, 4 seq.). They are shown with the Father and the Son. For the Apostle says that divine justification and spiritual law are fulfilled in these: not those who walk according to the flesh, but according to the Spirit. to be] and the works of the body, the Apostolic discourse described heavenly and eternal, and to deal with these things which are spirits. But the wisdom of the flesh, immediately associated with death, kills those who walk according to the flesh and are wise. all disturbances and kinds of vices, and even the demons themselves (who endeavor to suggest these things) will have under their feet. Therefore, if the wisdom of the flesh is united with death, it is hostile to God. For it makes enemies those who live by his laws: always contrary, and contrary to the will and the law for it is not possible for one who is in the wisdom of the flesh to keep the commandments of God and submit to his will. As long as we serve pleasures, we cannot serve God. in the flesh, that is, in the passions of the flesh, then shall we be subject to God. For not concerning this flesh in which we live, and in whose vessel our soul is contained, is the word of the Apostle, because all the saints, surrounded by body and flesh, have pleased God: but rather to that which is perpetrated against the commandment of God by human society, of whom it is said: You shall love the Lord your God (Deut. 6:5). but disciples of Christ, who have received the wisdom of the Spirit, and life and peace: you are not in the flesh, that is, in the works of the flesh, nor having done the works of it, for you have the Spirit of God in you. joining him who has in him to the Lord Jesus Christ. Whence and in the consequences, it is written: But if anyone does not have the Spirit of Christ, he is not his. in the Epistle of Peter, it is proved that the Holy Spirit is the Spirit of Christ: "Scrutinizing," he says, "and inquiring," that is, of the Prophets, about whom he had been spoken above, into what and what time he signified, who was in them the Spirit of Christ: bearing witness to the sufferings of Christ, and the decrees that were to follow after, in which it was revealed, that they ministered not to themselves, but to us, the things which have now been announced to you by the Holy Spirit (1 Pet. 1, 10 seq.). And this is called the Holy Spirit, and the Spirit of God, not only in the present discourse, but also in several other places, as there: The things of God no one knows but the Spirit of God (Rom. 8:9). this is not his, and it is inferred, but if Christ is in you, and it is most clearly demonstrated that the Holy Spirit is inseparable from Christ: for wherever the Holy Spirit is, there is Christ also, and from wherever the Spirit of Christ has departed, from there Christ also departs. For if anyone He does not have the Spirit of Christ, this is not his. If someone assumes the opposite of this, he can say: If someone is Christ, so that Christ is in him, the Spirit of God is in him. He does not have the Spirit of God; he is not his. Again, if anyone assumes the opposite, saying: If anyone is of God, the Spirit of God is in him. Whence it is written: You do not know that you are the temple of God, and that the Spirit of God dwells in you (1 Cor. 3, 16)? And in the letter of John: In this is known God dwelling in some, when the Spirit which he gave remained in them (1 John. iv, 2). Christ is in you, a body indeed dead because of sin (Rom. 8:10): never serving vices and lasciviousness, but mortified by sin, he is not moved to vices: and he will never be alive to sin. But after the body is dead to sin, Christ in those who have mortified their bodies, he shows the present Spirit of life through righteousness, whether the correction of the works of immortal virtues, or the faith of Jesus Christ, in those who are converted according to his faith. Then the apostle uses another conjunctive syllogism, which more significantly the dialecticians call ἀξίωμα, and he says: But if his Spirit which he raised Christ from the dead, he who raised Christ from the dead lives in you, he will also give life to your mortal bodies through his Spirit who dwells in you (Rom. 8:9): does it not seem to you that he is saying, because if the Spirit of him who raised Christ Jesus, that is , who is the same Spirit of Jesus Christ, dwells in you: consequently your mortal bodies will be quickened with immortal souls by him who raised Christ Jesus from the dead, the prince and firstborn of the resurrection? , not of the flesh, so that we may live according to it. For whoever lives according to the flesh will die that death which follows sin. Since sin, when it is consummated, generates death (James 1:15), according to James. But Ezekiel also writes that the sinning soul must die (Ezek 18). For it is already separated from the life which is placed in the wisdom of the Spirit. and it is called the Spirit of God. For if, he says, you live according to the flesh, you will die. But if by the Spirit you have mortified the deeds of the flesh, you will live (Rom. 8:13). , and consoling and challenging them to hope for better things, to whom he spoke, he said: For you did not again receive the spirit of slavery in fear: that is, not in the likeness of slaves, by fear and terror of punishments, keeping yourselves from vices: because you have the Spirit of adoption given to you by the Father, that is The Holy Spirit, who himself is called the Spirit, and of God, and of Christ, and of truth, and of wisdom. But if this Spirit adopts as sons of God those by whose condescension he becomes his inhabitant, I leave to you the understanding of the consequences of his power. cry out those who have had him, God the

THE HOLY GHOST

Father, as he shows in the speech saying: In which we cry Abba Father (Ibid. 15): by the same Spirit who adopts us as sons, bearing witness by his participation, which is possessed by our Spirit, because we are the children of God. The consequence of this is that God, as a father, has given us hereditary riches, spiritual gifts: but that we are joint heirs with Christ, that we are called his brothers by his grace and kindness. And we shall be heirs of God, and co-heirs with Christ if we sympathize: that we may also deserve to be glorified by the fellowship of his sufferings. containing the holy one, that we may be taught not only of the New, but also of the Old Testament, upon his faith and understanding. For we have already spoken above. in all the saints, both in those who were after the coming of our Lord, and also in the Patriarchs and Prophets, that is, the grace of the Holy Spirit was directed, and filled them with different charisms and virtues. , than even those who, after his coming, to raise the standard of justice, have obtained the knowledge of the truth; so also the Holy Spirit will inherit grace, because we have shown in many places above that the Holy Spirit is inseparable from the Father and the Son. bringing us according to his mercy, and according to the multitude of his justice. And he said: Are my people not children? and they shall not be transgressed. not a messenger, nor an angel, but he himself saved them: because he loved them and spared them. He himself redeemed them, and received them, and exalted them in all the days of the world. to enmity with them. He himself defeated them and remembered the days of old. Knowing that his grace and mercy were greater than what they had obtained by their own works, as if they were all speaking with one consent and concord in mind, I remembered the Lord's mercy. The virtues of the Lord are remembered, either of the miracles which he often wrought for them in the peoples, or of the departures of the soul, by which they were taught wholesome things through the Law, and the Prophets, and his precepts. Indeed, in the Scriptures the name of virtue signifies both. They say, in all that he repaid them, not according to his justice, but according to his mercy and goodness, who is the judge of the house of the seer, and of the worldly sense of the heart that sees the Lord. For it is true that torments and a tortured judge sometimes bring judgment to those who deserve it, yet he who looks deeper into the causes of things, seeing the purpose of his goodness, who desires to correct the sinner, confesses that good, saying. Bringing to us according to his mercy. For if the Lord attends to the iniquities of those whom he judges, who will endure? I go on to say that with the Lord there is propitiation: our Lord and Savior indeed brings us according to his mercy all things that advance us to salvation. and doing this in judgment, when he bestows upon us justice, which he bestowed upon us mixed with the goodness of mercy. both good and judge, and according to his mercy restoring his justice, and at the same time being good and just. God is written as good, and on the contrary, what they do not want, in the Epistle of Paul the Apostle (who is certainly a preacher of the New Testament) God is referred to as a just judge. There is laid up for me, he says, the crown of justice, which the Lord will give me on that day as a just judge (2 Tim. 4, 8). He is therefore the same, even if they do not want to, the God of the new and Old Testament, the creator of the visible and the invisible, the Savior also clearly attesting to the just and good Father in the Gospel: Righteous Father, the world has not known you (John. XVII, 11). in another place: There is no one good but one God (Mark 10:18). But in the old law, God is called righteous elsewhere, and God is called good. On the contrary, in Jeremiah, the Lord is good to those who support him. Again, in the Psalms, how good the God of Israel is to those who are upright in heart (Psal. 72:1). let us follow the purpose of the order of the Prophet, which is thus woven together: And he said, without doubt that the Lord, are not my people my children, and they shall not be transgressed (Isaiah 1:5)? They are called children; the cause of their salvation is the result. What salvation has been contributed by Christ the Lord, is also confirmed by the voice of the angels to the shepherds, saying: Behold, I bring you good tidings of great joy, which shall be to all people; because a Savior was born to you today, who is Christ the Lord, in the city of David (Luke 2:10). He is the one about whom the choir of saints sings: Our God, the God of salvation (Psal. 67). Moses the lawgiver did not save them. For all those whom I have named could act as ambassadors to the Lord on behalf of the people. Finally, Moses, addressing him on behalf of the delinquent people, said: If you forgive them their sin, forgive them (Exodus 32:31). But he begged forgiveness for forty days fasting, and provoking the mercy of God, by affliction of the soul. But none of these ambassadors can be a savior, being in need of him who is the true giver of salvation. They are sent, yet they are not the authors of salvation, but they interpret and sanctify him who is the source of salvation. He is said to spare them, as if to his own creatures, according to what is written elsewhere: But spare all, O Lord, lover of souls, because they are yours, for you do not hate those whom you have made (Sap. 11:29). The Father delivered him up to death, that by the death of his Son, having destroyed him who had the power of death, that is, the devil, he might redeem all who were held by him in the bonds of captivity. and exalts the saved, and lifts up the redeemed on high with the wings of virtue, and with learning and knowledge of the truth, not for one day only, and for another day, but in all the days of eternity, dwelling in them and with them, and giving them life and salvation until the end of the world But by enlightening their hearts all the days of the world, he does not allow them to dwell in the darkness of ignorance and error. they were unbelieving in God's favors, and forsook his precepts, and exasperated the Holy Spirit of God, who bestowed upon them many good things; they are described, for even there after the sin it is said to them: You forsook the Lord, and stirred up Holy Israel to anger, and now, because they did not believe and provoked his Holy Spirit. and he is unbelieving, and provokes Holy Israel to wrath, and exasperates his Holy Spirit. The same indignation against sinners is referred both to the Holy Spirit and to Holy Israel. Whence, and in the consequences, a similar coupling of the Trinity is shown, saying that the Lord turned to enmity with those who provoked his Holy Spirit, and delivered them up to eternal torment, after they had blasphemed his Holy Spirit, not by word, but by things. enmity, he defeated them and subjected them to multiple and long tortures, so that neither in the present time nor in the future they would obtain forgiveness of sins. For they aggravated his Holy Spirit and blasphemed against him. And therefore, they exasperated the Holy Spirit, what is written, He defeated them, is to refer to that intelligence, that they were handed over to the Romans, when the wrath of God came upon them to the end. Not possessing the ancient city, nor their own seats, they received what they did to the Prophets and to their Savior. They betrayed and crucified the Savior, who had deigned to come down to the earth for the salvation of all, and therefore they were expelled from the city, which they stained with the blood of the Prophets and of Christ. Therefore, according to this sense, we must understand them defeated by the Lord, not for a short time, but for all future ages until the consummation of the world. When (as we have said) the fugitives and captives wandered in all nations, possessing neither a city nor a country of their own. However, because He who had defeated them is naturally kind and merciful, He gives them a place of repentance, if they wish to turn to better things. Whence and it is said, He remembered the days of the age. For he remembered the times to come and opened a door that had been closed to them in some part, so that after the fullness of the nations had entered, then all Israel (who was worthy of this appellation) would be saved. had been sent, they would kill him, saying: His blood be on us and on our children (Matthew 27:25), yet God raised him from the earth, in whose heart he had dwelt three days and three nights: the shepherd of his sheep. He who brought forth from the earth the shepherd of his sheep (Isaiah 63:12).

49. That indeed the shepherd of the sheep, God, who is now described in prophetic language, is the Lord, we learn more clearly in the Gospel, by the Savior himself testifying, I am the good shepherd and I lay down my life for my sheep (John 10:11). And again, my sheep heard my voice. And he speaks in a certain way: He who redeemed them, who had placed his Holy Spirit in them, dwelling with them, where is he now? Where has he gone? God the Holy Spirit, when they were still good, and depended on obedience to his precepts. Worse things come together, they stir up against them their indweller, the Holy Spirit, and turn him who had given him to enmity. Something similar to this and the Apostle writing to the Thessalonians, says, For God has not called us to impurity, but to sanctification (1 Thess. 4, 7). that they should become believers, he gave them the Holy Spirit. And as long as they kept the commandments of God, the Holy Spirit remained in them, which they received. that they should serve uncleanness, but that they might be sanctified. Whence shall those who commit these things suffer punishments, not as men, but as blasphemers as God. mine is in thee, and I have put my words into thy mouth (Isaiah 16:21). God speaks instead of the same Prophet: I gave my Spirit upon him (Isa. 42, 1). He who then put the Holy Spirit in them, mentions that Moses was sanctified with his right hand: whether that illustrious man, and the initiator of the mysteries of God, about whom to Jesus the son of Mary said: Moses my servant, or his Law, which was written in the old Instrument. For I remember that I had often read that Moses was called the Law, as in the Apostle: Until this day, when Moses is read (II Cor. 3, 14). And Abraham was appointed to be rich in executions. They have, he says, Moses and the Prophets (Luke 16:29), if not the Lord and our Savior? For he is the right hand of the Father, through whom he saves and exalts and makes mighty, as it is said elsewhere of God: He saved his right hand and his holy arm (Psal. 107, 1). And again: The right hand of the Lord He has done strength, the right hand of the Lord has exalted me: I will not die, but live, and I will tell of the works of the Lord (Psal. 17:16). it is proved, because he is the right hand of God, as it is written in the Acts of the Apostles, that he was made of the seed of David according to the flesh, born of a virgin, the Holy Spirit coming upon her, and the power of the Most High overshadowing her. Of whom David prophesied

in the Spirit, that from the dead rising, let him be taken up into the heavens, lifted up by the right hand of God. And it is written there in this way: Foresight, the same David spoke of the resurrection of Christ, because he was not abandoned in hell, nor did his flesh see corruption. God raised up this Jesus, of whom we are all witnesses. Therefore, the right hand of God being lifted up, and receiving the promise of the Holy Spirit from the Father, he poured out this gift in us, which you see and hear, for David did not ascend into the heavens (Acts 2, 31 seq.). that the Lord Jesus was rising from the underworld, as he testified in the words of the Scriptures. Therefore, he who rose from the dead says: I slept and fell asleep, and rose again, because the Lord raised me up (Psal. 3:6). He is said to have been lifted up into heaven, from that of which we have spoken above, the right hand of God, and to have received the promises of the Holy Spirit from the Father, and to have poured it out on those who believe, so that the great things of God were spoken in all languages. It is written in the Gospels: Jesus therefore, filled with the Holy Spirit, returned from the Jordan (Luke 1:67). And in another place: Jesus returned in the power of the Spirit to Galilee (Luke 8:55). that the whole Christ, Jesus the Son of God, is one, we must accept with a sense of piety, not that there is one and the other, but that it is disputed about one and the same, as if about the other according to the nature of God and of man, and because God the Word is the only begotten Son of God, and neither changes receives, nor increases. For he is the fullness of all good things.

53. Enough has been discussed about the testimony of the Prophet, and let us not go on to the rest, so that how we know that the Father and the Son perfect the saints and the good by their communion: so also the Holy Spirit by his participation makes the good and the saints believers: and from this it is also taught that there is one substance with the Father and the Son. without any ambiguity it is called the good Spirit: You have given your good Spirit to make them understand (Ephesians 3:4). And what the Father sanctifies, the Apostle writes, saying: But the God of peace sanctifies you who are perfect. And the Savior says: Holy Father, sanctify them in truth, because your word is truth (John 17:11). Clearly saying: in me (who am your word and your truth), sanctify them by faith and my association. God (Luke 18:19). We also showed above that the Son will sanctify, agreeing with Paul in the same words: For he who sanctifies and those who are sanctified are all from one. Signifying Christ

who sanctifies, and those who are sanctified who can say, Wisdom has been made for us from God Christ, and righteousness, and sanctification (1 Cor.1, 30). He is indeed called the Spirit of sanctification. Whence it is said to him, and all those who are sanctified are under your hands and under you. Our good Lord Jesus Christ, and from He was begotten by a good Father, and we read about him, "Confidence in the Lord, for he is good" (Psal. 167, 1). And let those who either beg forgiveness of sins from him, or give thanks to his clemency for pardoning favors, also confide in those whom the Holy Spirit deigns to fulfill, sanctifies, as has already been demonstrated above, when we showed that it can be shared and taken by many at the same time. To the Lord, because God chose us as the first fruits for salvation, in the sanctification of the Holy Spirit, and in the faith of the truth (1 Thess. 2:13).

54. Therefore, because it is right and pious, and as the truth is, we have said these things, the term sanctification and goodness refer equally to the Father, and to the Son, and to the Holy Spirit, as also the very appellation of the Spirit. For the Father of the Spirit is also called, as there: Spirit is God (John 4:24). And the Son of the Spirit: the Lord, he says, is a Spirit (2 Cor. 3:17). But the Holy Spirit is always considered by the appellation of the Holy Spirit, not because the name Spirit is put together with the Father and the Son, but because it possesses one name and one nature. But since the term Spirit means many things, it is necessary to enumerate briefly the things to which its name is appropriate. It is called the Spirit and the wind, as in Ezekiel: And you shall scatter the third part into the spirit: that is, into the wind (Ezek. 5:2). But if you wish to understand according to history that which is written, in a violent spirit you would break the ships of Tharsis (Ps. 47:8), no other spirit is received there than the wind. Moreover, among many things, Solomon also received this gift from God, that he might know the violence of the spirits; showing that he had taken nothing else in this, then to know the swiftness of the winds, and by what causes their nature exists. The soul is also called the spirit, as in the Epistle of James: How thy body is dead without the spirit, and the rest (Jacob. II, 26). For most clearly the spirit here is called nothing else but the soul. According to the intelligence and Stephen, calling his soul his spirit, he says, Lord, Jesus, receive my spirit (Acts 7:58). Also, that which is said in Ecclesiastes: Who knows whether the spirit of a man ascends upwards, and the spirit of an animal descends downwards (Ecclesiastes 3:2)? Let us consider whether the soul and

the cattle are called spirits. It is also said that apart from the soul, and apart from our spirit, there is another Spirit in man, about whom Paul writes: For who knows the things of man, except the spirit of man, which is in him (1 Cor. 2:11)? For if he wishes to contend that any soul is here signified in the spirit, who will be the man whose thoughts, and the secret, and the hidden secrets of the heart, a man knows not except his spirit, because it is foolish to want to understand this from the isolated body.

55. But if the sly one endeavors to sneak in by fraud, disputing these things written about the Holy Spirit; if he carefully considers the words himself, he will cease to assert a lie. For it is thus written: For who knows the things of man, except the spirit of man, which is in him? Likewise, the things that are of God, no one knows, except the Spirit of God (1 Cor. 2:10). For just as man is different, God is different, so also the spirit of man, which is in him, is separated from the Spirit of God, which is in him: which we have frequently shown the Holy Spirit. But in another place the same apostle, separating the Spirit of God from our spirit, says, The Spirit Himself bears witness to our spirit (Rom. 8:16): signifying that the Spirit of God, that is, the Holy Spirit, bears witness to our spirit: which we have just said to be the Spirit of man. To the Thessalonians also: He says, your spirit, and soul, and body are whole (1 Thess. 5, 19). For just as the soul is different, and the body is different, so the spirit is also different from the soul, which is specially called in its place. About which he prayed that he may be preserved whole with soul and body, because it is incredible and blasphemous for the Apostle to pray that the Holy Spirit may be preserved whole, who can neither receive diminution nor depart. Therefore, as we have said, the Spirit testified in this speech of the Apostle.

56. The supernatural and rational virtues, which the Scriptures usually call angels and powers, are called by the word Spirit, as there: You make your angels spirits (Ps. 133:4). And elsewhere, Are not all stewards of the Spirit (Heb. 1:14)? I think that it is related to this sense and that which is written in the Acts of the Apostles: The Spirit of the Lord took Philip, and the eunuch saw him no more (Acts 8:39); that is, the angel of the Lord, raising Philip on high, transferred him to another place. Other creatures also rational and flowing from good to evil of their own accord, are called evil spirits and unclean spirits: as there: But when an unclean spirit comes out of a man. And in the

consequences: He assumed seven other spirits eviler than himself (Matthew 12:43). Spirits are also called demons in the Gospels. But this too is to be noted, that the spirit is never simply used, but with some addition the contrary spirit is signified, such as an unclean spirit, and the spirit of a demon; but those who are holy spirits are simply called spirits without any addition.

57. It must also be known that the name of the spirit sounds, and the will of man, and the opinion of the soul. For the Apostle, wishing that a virgin should be holy not only in work, but also in mind, that is, not only in body, but also in the inner movement of the heart, says, That she may be holy in body and in spirit (1 Cor. 7:34): the will is in the spirit, and the works in the body signifying Consider whether this sounds the same in Isaiah, which is written: And those who err in spirit shall know their understanding (Isaiah 29:24). For he who, by error of judgment, has other goods for others they think, they will receive the understanding, that their error may be corrected, that they may choose the things that are right instead of the wrong. And also, that, one strength of your Spirit, see if it shows the same thing. And above all, the word spirit signifies a higher and mystical understanding in the Holy Scriptures, as there: the letter kills, but the spirit gives life (2 Cor. 3:6); literally saying a simple and clear narrative next to history; but to know the spirit, the holy and the spiritual, what is read. The will and the saying agree with this: We are the circumcision, who serve the Lord in spirit, and do not trust in the flesh (Philippians 3:3). For those who do not circumcise the flesh in the letter, but circumcise the heart in the spirit, taking away all its excess, which is close to generation and a friend, these are truly circumcised in the spirit, in the secret of the Jews, and of the true Israelites, in whom there is no guile. Those who transcend the shadows and images of the Old Testament, the worshipers of truth, worship the Father in spirit and truth: in spirit, because they have transcended the corporeal and the lowly; in truth, because leaving types, and shadows, and models, they came to the substance of the truth itself: and, as we have already said, despised by the low and corporeal simplicity of words, they came to the spiritual knowledge of the law.

58. In the meantime, we have touched upon this, according to the possibility of our intellect, as many things as the spirit might signify, and in due time we will discuss what each one signifies, if Christ gives it. But sometimes the Spirit, and

our Lord Jesus Christ, that is, the Son of God, is called. Indeed, the Spirit of wisdom is kind. And in another place: But the Lord is a Spirit, as we said before, where we also added it, the Spirit is God (John 4:24), not only according to the communion of the name, but according to the association of nature and substance. For since their substance is different, it sometimes happens that they are called by a common term, and these are called ὁμώνυμα; Thus, those whose nature and substance are the same, with the association of the term, the equality of the nature also is joined, and it is the discipline of dialecticians to call these symbionts. For this reason, also the word Spirit, and if anything, else is usually used in the Trinity, it is συνώνυμον: for example, holy, good, and others similar to these, about which we have glimpsed a little before.

59. Furthermore, we are necessarily drawn to these things, so that since the appeal of the Spirit is frequently sprinkled in the Scriptures by the divine, we do not slip in the name, but take each according to the varieties and understandings of the places. Let us, therefore, with all diligence and care contemplate the word Spirit, where and how it is called, and destroy the sophistries and fraudulent disciples of those who assert that the Holy Spirit is a creature. For those who read in the Prophet, I am the one who strengthens the thunder and creates the Spirit (Amos, 4, 12), being ignorant of the multiples in this part of the speech, thought that the Holy Spirit was indicated by this term, when the name of the Spirit sounds in the presence of the Spirit. Moreover, hearing the Lord speak in Zechariah, that it is he who creates the spirit of man in him, they thought that the Holy Spirit was also signified in this chapter, not noticing that the appellation of spirit signifies the soul of man, or the spirit (which we have already said is the third in man). Therefore, as we have already spoken, let us consider how each one was said, lest through ignorance we should fall into the trap of error. Indeed, in other matters the error resulting from the association of terms implies confusion and shame to him who has erred: from the heavenly truth and the divine fall he leads to perversity, to eternal punishment, and to the Tartarus, especially when once he has been deceived, he will not repent, but shamelessly defends his error. It was also fitting, and the size of the volume demanded that the speech should end.

60. But since a question arises against what we have discussed above, which we then passed over, lest the text of the discourse should be interrupted, and an

impious contention should be placed between the pious preaching, I think it necessary to answer the purpose, and to leave to the discretion of the reader what he may think about them. Therefore, to those arguing above, that no creature can fill the soul or mind of man according to substance, except the Trinity alone, because only according to the operation, and the error of the will, or the power, is the mind filled with the things that have been created: our question has arisen, as if solving the sentence, that the created substance, which in the Scriptures is called Satan, enters into some, and is said to fill the hearts of some. For to him who kept half the price of the land sold to himself, claiming otherwise, Peter the Apostle said, Ananias, why has Satan filled your heart (Actor. 5, 3)? And the Savior himself speaks of Judas, that Satan entered into him. To which we must answer later. Meanwhile, let us now argue against what is written, Why has Satan filled your heart? how Satan fills the mind of any one and the principal of the heart, not entering into him and his sense, and, so to speak, entering the access of the heart: for this power belongs to the Trinity alone; He draws the affections of malice, through the thoughts and incentives of the vices with which he is full. Finally, Elymas himself, the sorcerer, the son of the devil, subsisting next to malice and wickedness, full of all deceit and malice, is written Satan his Father, turning this will to him, as if from the habit of vices into nature. Therefore, the Apostle Paul, accusing him and rebuking him, said: O full of all iniquity and all deceit, son of the devil, enemy of the justice of God (Acts 13:10)! For because he was sly and cunning and had taken up in himself every trick of fraud, he is called the son of the devil, because he himself filled all his chieftains with fraud and iniquity, and with all malice; whom he had prepared as his minister and servant for all the tricks of his perversity.

61. In regard to the fact that we set the second example, because Satan had entered into Judah, this must be said. Observing certain movements and signs of operations, to which the heart of Judas was most prone to vice, the devil found him open to the snares of avarice, and finding the door of covetousness, sent into his mind how he might get the desired money, and through the opportunity of profit, to exist as a traitor to his Master and Savior, silver exchanging for piety, and accepting the price of crime from the Pharisees and Jews. This occasion of thought, then, gives place to Satan, who, entering into his heart, fills him with the worst will. He entered, therefore, not according to

substance, but according to operation; for to enter into any one is of his uncreated nature, which is shared by many. Therefore, the devil is incomparable, not a creator, but a subsisting creature. Hence, both convertible and changeable, he falls from sanctity and virtue. We said above that μετοχικὸν, that is, that which is taken by participation, is incorruptible and unchangeable, and consequently eternal. But what can be changed must be a fact and have a beginning. Moreover, that which is incorruptible, is eternal both backward and forward. It is not therefore (as some think) that the devil fills any substance by participating in nature or substance, or becomes its inhabitant, but through fraud, deception, and malice, he is believed to dwell in that which he has filled. And this deception also entered into the priests, who had turned to cruelty against Susanna: filling their souls with the burning of lust, and the late pleasure of old age. For it is written: And there came also two priests, full of unrighteous thought (Dan., 13:28). He also filled the entire Jewish people with these snares, the Prophet saying about him: Woe to the sinful nation, the people full of sins, the worst seed, the sons of the wicked (Isaiah 1:4). For the evil seed, the devil, and his children, because of their iniquity and fullness, were called sinners. But if by those who are named his sons in the Scriptures, he is not apprehended according to the participation of substance, since it has been frequently shown that this is impossible in creatures, no one else can apprehend him by the participation of substance, but only by the assumption of the most fraudulent will. For we have spoken of working and studying not only good works, but also evil ones in creatures; but the nature and substance of the Trinity can enter only into others.

62. Abundantly (as I think) there is an encounter with the proposed question. But because it seems foolish and foolish to reply against foolish things, and if anything rushes into the mouths of the wicked, to want to dissolve it; for it is not so much impiety to set forth the wicked, as to wish to deal with the wicked when they are resisting: therefore I pass over that which they are wont to hurl, boldly proclaiming sacrilegious things against us: If the Holy Ghost was not created, he is either the brother of God the Father, or the uncle of the only begotten Jesus of Christ, either he is the son of Christ, or he is the grandson of God the Father, or he himself is the son of God, and the Lord Jesus Christ will no longer be the only begotten, since he has another brother. The wretched and pitiful, not feeling that the nature of the incorporeal and the invisible should

not be allowed to be discussed next to the corporeal and the visible. To be a brother or an uncle, a nephew or a son, are names of bodies, and terms of human weakness. But Trinity transcends all these names. And every time he falls into any of these: he does not speak of his nature in our names, and in incongruous terms. Therefore, since the Holy Scriptures say no more about the Trinity, except that God is the Father of the Savior, and that the Son was begotten by the Father, we must only understand what is written. And if I show that the Holy Spirit is uncreated, we must consequently understand that whose substance is not created, he is rightly associated with the Father and the Son.

63. In accordance with the poverty of our discourse, let these things be sufficient for the present: they indicate my fear, that I have dared to speak of the Holy Spirit. For whoever blasphemes against him, not only in this world, but also in the future, he will not be forgiven, nor will any mercy and pardon be reserved for him who has trampled on the Son of God and has done an injury to the Spirit of his grace, in which he was sanctified. This, indeed, is to be understood in God the Father. For he who has blasphemed against him and acted impiously, will be tortured without forgiveness, with no one supplicating the Lord for him, as it is written, but he who has sinned against the Lord God, who will pray for him? And he who denies the Son before men will be denied by him before the Father and his angels. Therefore, since no forgiveness is granted to those who blaspheme the Trinity, we must take care with all diligence and caution, so that we do not slip in discussing it even in short, small talk. Rather, if anyone wishes to read this volume, we ask that he cleanse himself from all evil deeds and worst thoughts: so that he can understand with an enlightened heart what is said, and full of sanctity and wisdom, forgive us, if the result did not fulfill our will, and only let him consider with what mind what was said, not by what words it was expressed. For just as we boldly claim for ourselves the sense of piety next to our conscience, so far as it pertains to talk about it, we simply confess that the beauty and eloquence of rhetoric, according to the consequence and text of the speech, are far off. For it was our study, discussing the holy Scriptures, to piously understand what was written, and not to be ignorant of our incompetence and measure of speech.

THE HOLY GHOST

The Scriptorium Project is the work of a small group of lay people of various apostolic churches who are interested in the preservation, transmission, and translation of the works of the early and medieval church. Our efforts are to make the works of the church fathers accessible to anyone who might have an interest in Christian antiquities and the theological, philosophical, and moral writings that have become the bedrock of Western Civilization.

To-date, our releases have pulled from the Greek, Syriac, Georgian, Latin, Celtic, Ethiopian, and Coptic traditions of Christianity, and have been pulled from sundry local traditions and languages.

THE HOLY GHOST

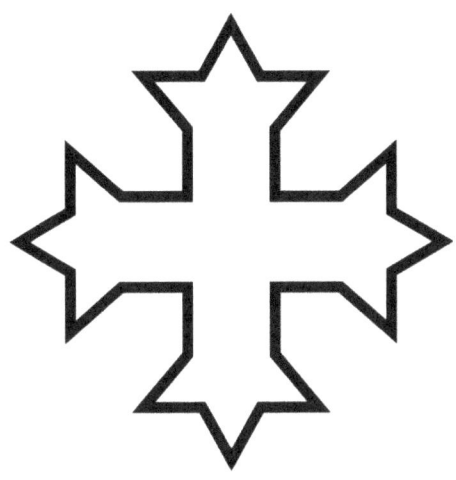

Nile River Valley Church Series (Coptic, Nubian, Ethiopian):

The Holy Ghost by St. Didymas the Blind (Sept. 2008)
The Paradise of Heraclides by Heraclides of Alexandria (Apr. 2013)
Discourse on Mary Theotokos by St. Cyril of Jerusalem (Sept. 2013)
Nicene Canons in the Old Nubian Language (Jan. 2018)
First Book of Ethiopian Maccabees (Dec 2018)
Life of St. Mary the Egyptian by St. Sophronius of Jerusalem (May 2019)
The Old Nubian Miracle of St. Mena (Jan. 2021)
Two Letters by St. Dionysius of Alexandria (Apr. 2022)
Instructions: Counsel for Novices by St. Ammonas the Hermit (Sept 2022)
Religious Exercise and Quiet by St. Isaiah the Solitary (Oct 2022)
The Vision of Theophilus by St. Cyril of Alexandria (Dec 2022)
Second Book of Ethiopian Maccabees (Aug 2023)

THE HOLY GHOST

www.ingramcontent.com/pod-product-compliance
Lightning Source LLC
LaVergne TN
LVHW051921060526
838201LV00060B/4122